Thinking Games 1

Valerie Anderson
Carl Bereiter
with the assistance of
Kathy Fry and Arlene Kaplan

Fearon Teacher Aids
Carthage, Illinois

Cover design: Susan True
Revision editing: Leigh Blair
Illustrations: Rod Della-Vedova, Mary Ann Schildknecht

This book was originally published as *Thinking Games, Book 1*, by the Ontario Institute for Studies in Education. The material is republished in this United States edition by agreement with the Ontario Institute.

ISBN-0-8224-6941-3
Library of Congress Catalog Card Number 79-57429
Printed in the United States of America
1. 9

Contents

GAMES FOR LARGER GROUPS

Introduction

Thinking games are designed for children to have fun while exercising their thinking abilities. The games in this book give practice in such skills as planning, drawing inferences, seeing things from other points of view, formulating questions, and thinking of possibilities.

There are already a number of good thinking games available for children to play — chess, Monopoly, Clue, etc., and even hide-and-seek, which involves some planning, originality, and seeing things from another person's point of view. This book supplies fifty-four new games, and its companion volume, *Thinking Games 2,* supplies sixty-four more. There were several reasons for creating these new games. The most obvious reason is that children can profit from having many more games available. Not every child likes or has a talent for chess. Other strategy games are needed to provide a range of choices. Moreover, no single game teaches very much. As you play chess you may improve your planning abilities a little bit, but mostly you just become better at playing chess. And so it is with every game.

The games in this book differ from many others in that they are cheap (they either require no special materials or ones that you can easily obtain yourself) and the rules are easy to learn. We have also tried to design the games to avoid dog-eat-dog competition. There is enough competition to generate excitement, but it is frequently competition between teams rather than individuals.

All the games have been thoroughly tested and revised, with different groups of children, so that you can be reasonably sure they will work with children of the appropriate ages. There are quiet games and active games, games for two and games for a classroom-size group to play at once. There are games for all levels of sophistication, including some that adults may enjoy. Games are grouped according to the number of players, and **within each group the first games are for younger children and the later, more challenging games, are for older children.**

Primarily the games were designed for use in school. They can be introduced at odd moments or made a regular part of the curriculum. In try-out schools children played games for about an hour a week, on the average. Some teachers supervised the games rather closely. Others introduced the games and then let children play them independently while other classroom activities were going on. The games can be used equally well at home or with other children's groups.

We have some research evidence to show that children who play the games regularly over the span of a school year improve in creative thinking skills and in their ability to participate in group problem-solving. Some teachers have reported improvements in reasoning abilities, but we have no evidence that this is a typical result. Our guess is that children will have to play thinking games for several years before any basic improvements in reasoning skills will become apparent. But even that is a speculation. The strongest reason, after all, for encouraging children to play thinking games is not to improve their minds but to let them experience the joy of using their minds in play.

CARL BEREITER

Games for small groups

Radar

SKILLS: CODING (NONVERBAL).

A player with a bag over his head uses information that other players give him to draw a line to a small circle on the chalkboard.

Players: 3 or more.
Materials: Chalkboard, chalk, and a large paper bag.

Game Procedure
1. A player is chosen who places a paper bag over his head.
2. He is given a piece of chalk and led to the chalkboard.
3. The other players sit facing the chalkboard.
4. One player draws a small circle anywhere on the board, keeping its location secret from the player wearing the bag, then sits down.
5. The player wearing the bag draws a line on the chalkboard and tries to reach the circle that has been drawn.
6. The other players guide him by giving "radar" beeps, beeping slowly when the line is far from the circle and faster as the line comes nearer to the circle.
7. When the circle has been reached, the player wearing the bag chooses another player to wear it, and the game begins again.

Special Considerations
Before playing the game for the first time, players may need practice in beeping slowly and quickly at the right times. Emphasize that beeping should become faster rather than louder.

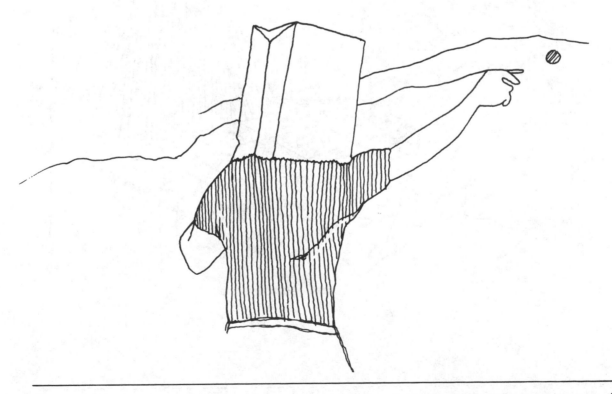

2

SKILLS: STRATEGY.

Ordinary Tic-Tac-Toe is expanded in size and in the range of possible playing strategies.

Players: 2.
Materials: Paper and pencil for each player.

Game Procedure

1. The game begins with a grid like ordinary Tic-Tac-Toe but bigger, with five squares in each row.

2. Each player chooses an X or an O as his mark.
3. Players take turns making their marks, one square per turn.
4. The first player to complete a row, column, or diagonal wins.

Sentence Tic-Tac-Toe

SKILLS: STRATEGY, VERBAL ORGANIZATION.

Two players try to win a row of squares on a matrix by making sentences from pairs of words.

Players: 2.
Materials: Paper and pencil for each player.

Game Procedure
1. Each player secretly prints four words.
2. A player draws a simple matrix of four spaces across and down (as shown).
3. One player prints his words above the four spaces across the top.
4. The other player prints his words by the four spaces down the side.
5. Each player chooses X or O as his mark.
6. Players take turns trying to win squares on the board.
7. To win a square, a player must be able to use the words above and beside that square in one complete sentence. For example, to win the lower-right-hand square on the board shown, a player would have to make a complete sentence using the words *fight* and *school*, such as, "You shouldn't fight in school."
8. A player puts his mark in a square when he wins it.
9. If a player cannot make a sentence, he cannot mark a square.
10. The first player to complete a row, column, or a diagonal wins the game.

	dog	run	play	school
man				
house				
jump				
fight				

SKILLS: ORIGINALITY, LANGUAGE, READING.

Players try to think of one use for three different objects.

Players: 3 or 4.

Materials: Fifteen index cards with one of the following objects drawn or cut out and pasted onto each card: newspaper, tree, fireplace, milk, bottle, glasses, stove, sled boot, book, sofa, coat, pan, paintbrush, table.

Game Procedure

1. Players sit facing each other or in a circle.
2. One player is chosen to be dealer.
3. The dealer gives three cards to each player and three to himself.
4. The dealer begins the game by naming the objects on his three cards.
5. He then tries to think of one way to use all three things on his cards. For example, if his cards are a pair of glasses, a sofa, and a book, he could say, "Someone might wear glasses and sit on the sofa to read a book." This would be correct because he would be using all three things to do one specific thing: read a book.
6. If the answer is correct, the dealer may throw a card of his choice into the center of the circle.

7. If the answer is incorrect or the dealer cannot answer, he must keep all three cards.
8. The player to the right of the dealer continues in the same way.
9. When each player has had a turn, he chooses one of his three cards and passes it to the player on his right for the second round.
10. Each player again tries to think of some way to use all of his cards. Some players will still be working with three cards; those who were able to discard on their first turn will only have two.
11. The game continues in this way with players discarding one card for a correct reply and passing a card to the player on the right for each new round.
12. The first player to discard all of his cards is the winner. The game may continue if players wish to determine second and third place winners.

Special Considerations

It should be emphasized that the three cards must be used for one thing. Players may name three different things they could do with each of the cards, but this problem usually disappears after one round of the game.

Make Twenty

SKILLS: RECOGNIZING PROGRESS TOWARD A SOLUTION, ARITHMETIC (ADDITION).

Players draw and play number cards until they total exactly twenty.

Players: 2 or 4.

Materials: Forty-five index cards with a single number on each card. There should be five of each of the numbers from one to nine. Ordinary playing cards may be used, but require separating the aces (for one) and the twos through nines from more than one deck (for five sets of all numbers).

Game Procedure

1. Two players sit facing each other with the shuffled deck of number cards between them.
2. Each player draws two cards from the deck.
3. Each player must play one card at a time, face-up, until the numbers on the cards total exactly twenty.
4. The first player plays one of his cards, then draws another from the deck.
5. The other player plays a card, then draws another from the deck.
6. Players take turns playing and drawing a card until someone has played cards that total twenty.
7. If a player's draw makes his cards total more than twenty, he must discard and wait to draw again.
8. The first player whose cards total twenty with a discard wins the round.
9. All cards played during the round are put in the discard pile.
10. The game continues until all cards in the deck have been used.
11. The player who has won the most rounds wins the game.

Variations

The game may include four players by doubling the number of cards.

6

Buy a Guess

SKILLS: EDUCATED GUESSING, RECOGNIZING PROGRESS TOWARD A SOLUTION, COMPARING, ARITHMETIC (MORE AND LESS).

Two players try to guess each other's secret number, but each guess must be "paid for."

Players: 2.

Materials: Forty slips of paper or other counters to be used as money.

Game Procedure

1. The money is divided equally between the players.
2. One player begins as leader.
3. He secretly writes a number larger than one and smaller than one hundred, then asks the other player to guess it.
4. The second player guesses a number and pays the leader one piece of "money" for the guess.
5. The leader raises his hand above his shoulder if the secret number is higher than the guess or lowers it below his waist level if the secret number is lower than the guess.
6. The second player continues to guess and pay until he narrows down the number enough to guess it.
7. The second player becomes leader, writes a secret number, and so on.
8. If a player runs out of money before he guesses the secret number, the leader wins, the money is divided anew, and the other player becomes leader.

9. More often, no one runs out of money, so the players can stop at any point that is fair, for example, after two, four, or six turns each as leader, as long as both have had the same number of turns.
10. The player with the most money at the stopping point is the winner.

Special Considerations

A player seldom runs out of money on one turn. If this happens, it means that the game is probably too advanced and that he has used pure guesswork which isn't very much fun.

Some younger players do not know whether 62 is more than 49. An adult should monitor the first game to determine whether both players are qualified. However, he should not explain the strategy of narrowing the number down, since the thinking value of the game lies in the players' discovery of this strategy.

If a player doesn't know the sequence of larger numbers well enough to operate in the range of 1–100, he should play first in the range of 1–10 with only five pieces of money per player, or in a range of 1–30 with only ten pieces of money per player. He may also need to have a vertical number line drawn on the board.

Beginner's Hunch

SKILLS: CLASSIFYING, EDUCATED GUESSING, STRATEGY, LANGUAGE, READING.

Players make moves on a board to match a verb with a man-made or living thing.

Players: 2, 3, or 4.

Materials: A playing board larger than the one shown on this page may be drawn on heavy cardboard. Any small objects, such as pennies, buttons, or bottle-caps, may be used for tokens. Two decks of cards made from 2" x 2" squares of colored construction paper are also required. Each deck has thirty cards. All cards in one deck should be one color; all cards in the other should be another color. One deck should have the name of one of the following man-made objects printed on each card: truck, spoon, thread, stove, button, saw, pot, stairs, hat,

START

hear	stand	sew	eat	jump	build
ride	hop	fly	roar	hunt	play
color	shout	wash	tie	crawl	drive
sit on	dance	hide	cook with	lift	paint
smell	read	wear	write	talk	sit

FINISH

pitcher, pencil, hammer, paper, pen, elevator, car, kettle, bowl, knife, cloth, book, ball, needle, coat, soap, string, chair, match, faucet, shovel.

The other deck should have the name of one of the following living things printed on each card: weed, dog, flower, baby, lion, bat, frog, girl, kangaroo, cat, boy, giraffe, alligator, tiger, wolf, bear, seal, monkey, fly, bee, elephant, snake, camel, worm, penguin, man, canary, plant, cow, horse.

Game Procedure
1. Players sit around the board.
2. Each player chooses a token.
3. All players begin at the point marked "Start" on the board.
4. Players take turns, moving one square in any direction, if possible.
5. Before making a move, a player draws a card from either the man-made or the living deck.
6. Before drawing, a player should consider all of his available spaces to see if more of those verbs apply to living or man-made things. His choice of decks should be based on that consideration.
7. If he draws a man-made card, he must move to a square with a verb describing what the object on the card is used for. For example, if he draws "pen" he may move to a square with "color" or "write."

8. If he draws a living card, he must move to a square with a verb describing what the thing does. For example, if he draws the word "cat" he may move to a square with "eat" or "sleep."
9. A player must move if he can, even if it means moving backward.
10. He cannot move to a space occupied by another player.
11. He may move in any direction, but never more than one space per turn.
12. If a player cannot move because he has no suitable verb to move to, he loses his turn, stays where he is and tries again on the next turn.
13. The first player to reach the finish area is the winner. He is declared winner when he moves to the space next to the finish area.

Special Considerations
Players may choose a deck indiscriminately at first. They should be reminded to look at all the spaces to which they could move, then choose the deck to which most of the available verbs apply. It also should be pointed out that some of the verbs, such as "eat," "write," and others may apply to both decks, depending upon the word drawn.

Definition Card Game

SKILLS: DEFINING, READING, LANGUAGE.

Players must decide whether their cards provide a complete definition. Reading is required.

Players: 3 to 8.

Materials: A set of fifty index cards. A list of animal attributes is found at the end of this game. One attribute should be copied onto each card in the set. A list of food attributes and household furnishing attributes are also found at the end of the game. These can be used on additional sets of cards for variations of the same game.

Game Procedure

1. Players sit at a table or in a circle on the floor.
2. A player is chosen to deal four cards to each player.
3. The other cards are put in the middle of the playing area.

4. The dealer determines whether one or more of his cards describe a single animal to the exclusion of any other animal.
5. If not, he draws another card and passes to the next player.
6. If so, he puts down the defining cards, reads them aloud, states the animal he thinks they define, then asks to be challenged; for example, "It has wings, and it is brightly colored, so it's a parrot. Could it be anything else?"
7. If the players cannot think of another animal that fits that description, the cards stay down and the next player continues.
8. If another player can think of something else, such as "cardinal," the definer must pick up his cards again and draw another card before the next player continues.
9. Once a player has displayed an adequate definition, he may take his turn either by putting down a new definition or by adding some attributes to other players' definitions, but he may not do both on the same turn.
10. A player may pass and draw one card if he does not wish to play.
11. If a player includes an attribute that does not apply in his definition and is caught, he picks up his cards and draws a card.

12. If a player inaccurately adds to another player's definition, he must pick up his cards and draw a card.
13. Definitions may include as many cards as the player can appropriately apply.
14. The first player to get rid of all his cards is the winner.

Special Considerations

If an attribute card seems to create particular ambiguities for the players, it is best to discard it. Fifty cards are not essential to the game. If all cards have been used before any player has used all of his cards and if someone cannot play the cards left in his hand, the player with the fewest cards would be the winner.

Younger players may need extra guidance in the game until all the rules are learned. The most common problems of younger players are failing to use more than one card to make a definition and producing definitions that are easily challenged. Being challenged a few times, however, solves these problems and the players begin to seek more adequate card combinations. An adult can help prevent these problems when the game is introduced by demonstrating good definitions that use two or three cards and by showing examples of definitions that are easy to challenge.

Older players may find that the game ends too quickly, particularly if they are very good at playing single cards on other players' definitions. This may be solved by allowing a player to add only one card to an existing definition on each turn, or by allowing players to change a definition when they add to it and thus block the moves that subsequent players may have planned. For example, if a display for "walrus" included the cards "It lives where it is very cold," "It eats fish," and "It swims," the player may add, "It is always white," and change the definition to a "polar bear."

When introducing the game, the adult may feel that the players miss seemingly obvious opportunities to challenge. For example, "It has spots and it looks like a cat, so it's a leopard," may go unchallenged although it could easily be challenged by "cheetah." Such oversights may be simply a lack of knowledge and are better discussed at another time. More obvious oversights such as "It has stripes, so it's a tiger," with no mention that it could be a zebra, may represent lack of thought and should be pointed out.

Animal Attribute Cards

IT HAS WINGS.

IT LIVES WHERE IT IS VERY COLD.

IT EATS FISH.

IT CAN WORK AT THE CIRCUS.

IT SWIMS A LOT.

IT SLEEPS MOST OF THE WINTER.

IT LOOKS LIKE A CAT.

THE BABY IS CALLED A CUB.

IT ALWAYS HAS STRIPES.

IT IS ALWAYS BLACK AND WHITE.

IT HAS CLAWS.

IT HAS A VERY LONG NECK.

IT HAS HOOVES.

A PERSON CAN RIDE ON IT.

IT TALKS.

IT SLEEPS IN A BARN.

IT HAS FEATHERS.

IT IS ALWAYS WHITE.

IT HAS A TRUNK.

IT LIKES TO HOLD UP A BALL
    WITH ITS NOSE.

IT HAS FUR.

IT HAS A MANE ON ITS NECK.

IT ROARS.

IT GROWLS.

IT ALWAYS HAS SPOTS.

IT IS USUALLY BROWN.

IT LOOKS LIKE A HORSE.

IT LIVES ON A FARM.

IT LIKES TO EAT GRASS.

IT SINGS.

IT EATS NUTS.

IT HAS A LONG TAIL.

IT HAS WHISKERS.

IT LIVES IN A TREE.

IT HAS A BEAK.

IT SAYS MOO.

IT HAS A SHORT TAIL.

IT IS VERY BIG.

IT SAYS QUACK QUACK.

IT CAN FLY.

IT HAS LONG EARS.

IT HAS A SNOUT.

IT HAS BRIGHT COLOURS.

IT HAS HORNS.

IT GIVES PEOPLE THE MILK THEY DRINK.

IT LIVES IN THE WOODS.

IT IS VERY SMALL.

IT LIVES WHERE IT IS VERY HOT.

IT IS OFTEN A HOUSE PET.

IT HAS A BIG MOUTH.

Food Attribute Cards

IT IS ALWAYS BROWN.

THE PART WE EAT GROWS
    UNDERGROUND.

IT IS WRINKLED.

IT IS A DRINK.

IT HAS A BRIGHT PEEL.

IT GROWS IN A BUNCH.

IT IS OFTEN PURPLE.

IT IS MADE FROM MILK.

MONKEYS EAT THEM.

WE GET IT FROM COWS OR CATTLE.

IT IS ALWAYS YELLOW.

IT IS MEAT.

IT IS THICK AND CREAMY.

IT IS ALL GREEN.

IT IS ALWAYS WHITE.

IT TASTES SALTY.

IT IS CRUNCHY.

WE GET IT FROM A BIRD.

MICE LIKE IT.

IT MUST BE COOKED FIRST.

IT GROWS ON A TREE.

IT IS A VEGETABLE.

IT IS OFTEN RED.

IT IS SOUR.

BABIES DRINK IT.

WE EAT IT ESPECIALLY AT CHRISTMAS.
WE PUT IT IN SALADS.
WE GET IT FROM PIGS.
IT COMES IN A BOTTLE.
IT IS PARTLY GREEN.
SOME PEOPLE PUT SUGAR IN IT.
WE PUT MILK ON IT.
WE BUY IT IN BAGS.
WE CATCH IT IN WATER.
IT IS OFTEN FRIED.
IT MAY BE EATEN COOKED OR RAW.
IT HAS A VERY STRONG SMELL.
IT MAKES A GOOD DESSERT.
IT IS SWEET.
IT HAS A SHELL.
CATS EAT IT.
IT HAS STRIPES.
IT IS EATEN COLD.
IT COMES ON A STICK.
IT IS ROUND.
IT TASTES GOOD WITH EGGS.
WE BUY AND EAT IT AT THE MOVIES.
WE OFTEN DRINK IT IN THE MORNING.
IT IS ALWAYS ORANGE.
IT IS A FRUIT.
WE PUT IT ON A BUN.
IT COMES IN SECTIONS.

Household Furnishing Attribute Cards

IT HAS FOUR LEGS.
WE SLEEP ON IT.
IT IS OFTEN WHITE.
WE PUT CLOTHES IN IT.
IT IS ALWAYS HARD.
WE LIKE TO WATCH IT.
IT IS BIG.
IT HANGS ON THE WALL.
IT IS USUALLY BROWN.
IT IS MADE OF METAL.

IT PLAYS MUSIC.
IT IS IN THE KITCHEN.
IT CAN BE VERY HOT.
IT HAS DIALS.
IT IS OFTEN SOFT.
IT HAS ARMS.
IT HAS A BACK.
IT IS COLD INSIDE.
IT IS MADE OF WOOD.
IT IS LONG.
WE USE IT TO HOLD BOOKS.
IT IS IN THE DINING ROOM.
IT WORKS WHEN IT IS PLUGGED IN.
THREE PEOPLE CAN SIT ON IT.
PEOPLE PUT A BASE ON IT.
IT HAS A DOOR.
IT HAS DRAWERS.
IT HELPS US KEEP CLEAN.
WE OFTEN PUT A CLOTH ON IT.
IT IS PARTLY MADE OF CLOTH.
ONLY ONE PERSON SITS ON IT.
WE CAN TURN IT OFF.
IT IS IN THE LIVING ROOM.
WE EAT ON IT.
IT CAN BE VERY BRIGHT.
IT HAS SPRINGS.
A BABY USES IT, GROWN-UPS DO NOT.
IT MAY HAVE CUSHIONS ON IT.
IT MAY HAVE MORE THAN FOUR LEGS.
IT CAN BE ROUND.
IT HAS SHELVES.
IT CAN MOVE BACK AND FORTH.
YOU CAN HEAR IT.
YOU CAN PUT A LAMP ON IT.
IT HOLDS WATER.
IT IS SMALL ENOUGH TO LIFT EASILY.
IT HAS HANDLES.
IT IS IN THE BEDROOM.
WE CAN WRITE ON IT.
WE CAN POLISH IT.

Games for 5~12 players

Touch and Tell

SKILLS: IMAGERY, EDUCATED GUESSING.

A blindfolded player must recognize other players by touch.

Players: 5 to 12.
Materials: A blindfold.

Game Procedure
1. Players form a large circle.
2. One player is chosen to be blindfolded in the center of the circle.
3. The rest of the players walk to the right so that the player in the center will not know their positions in the circle.
4. The blindfolded player walks forward with his arms outstretched until he touches someone.
5. He continues to touch the person until he can guess who it is.
6. He gets two chances to guess.
7. Whether he is correct or incorrect, the person he has touched is next to be blindfolded in the center of the circle.

Special Considerations
Some players need to be reminded that they can touch the person's face and hair, as well as their body, before they guess who it is. It is also important to stress that players be extremely quiet so that they do not give away their identity by the sound of their voice or laughter. It is often interesting to ask children how they could tell who they were touching.

Variations
The game may also be played in a large open area. One player is blindfolded as above and the others scatter themselves about the room in simple hiding places. When the blindfolded player finds someone, he must guess who it is by touching, and that person is next to be blindfolded.

What's Next?

SKILLS: COMPLETING AND CONTINUING, SEQUENCING, LANGUAGE.

Players must be able to continue a song from where the previous player left off.

Players: 5 to 12.
Materials: None.

Game Procedure

1. Players stand and form a circle.
2. One player is chosen as leader who stands inside the circle.
3. The leader chooses a song that the entire group knows well.
4. One player is chosen to begin singing the song.
5. At any time, the leader taps the singing player on the head and the next player (clockwise) must continue the song from where the first player stopped.
6. When the leader taps the second player on the head, the next player continues, etc.
7. Players take turns around the circle continuing the song from wherever it is temporarily stopped by the leader.
8. To stay in the game, a player must stop singing immediately when tapped on the head. Once a player stops singing, the next player must continue the song appropriately with the next word after the last word sung.
9. Players who do not stop when tapped or who do not continue the song appropriately must sit down in the center of the players' circle.
10. If a player has to sit down, the next player must continue for him or also sit down.
11. The leader is the final judge of whether a player may stay in the game.
12. The last player standing is the winner and becomes the leader for the next round.

Special Considerations

When a player cannot continue the song, it is unlikely that the next player will be able to continue. Particularly when the game is first introduced, a number of players may have to sit down rather quickly. This is not serious at first because it speeds up the game. Players soon become better at attending to what has been sung and the problem disappears.

It may be difficult to find songs that the entire group knows. Practice a song with the players so that it is memorized before using it in the game. Familiar poems or nursery rhymes also may be used. For younger players, the game may be introduced with the alphabet or alphabet song.

Find Your Partner

SKILLS: EDUCATED GUESSING, PERCEPTUAL ORGANIZATION.

Players try to recognize shapes by touch rather than by sight.

Players: 5 to 12.
Materials: Pairs of different shapes, with a different pair for each player. These may be made by the class from heavy construction paper. They need not be traditional geometric shapes.

Game Procedure

1. Each player gets a matching pair of shapes.
2. Players form a large circle.
3. One player, *It*, is asked to leave the room.
4. A leader is chosen who takes one shape from each player.
5. *It* returns and stands in the circle with his hands behind him.
6. The leader secretly chooses a shape from those collected and puts it into *It*'s hands. *It* must hold the shape behind his back so he can't see it.
7. All players hold up their shapes.
8. By only feeling the shape behind his back, *It* must find the shape from those in the circle that is exactly like his.
9. He may choose three times before being shown the shape that is like his.
10. The person holding the matching shape is next to leave the room for a new game.

Special Considerations

If the game is too difficult, it may be played with pairs of objects found in the classroom.

If the game is too easy, some pairs of shapes may differ from others only in size. For example, one player may hold a large triangle while another holds a small triangle. Another way to make the game difficult is to have players cover part of their shapes as they hold them up.

12

SKILLS: GENERATING POSSIBILITIES, PLANNING.

Teams challenge each other to show the actions they can perform while balancing an eraser somewhere on their body, but they can't ask the opposition to do something that they can't do themselves.

Players: 4 to 12.
Materials: Chalkboard erasers.

Game Procedure

1. Players form two equal teams with opposing players paired off and facing each other.
2. The first player (Team A) asks his opposition (Team B) if he can perform an action while balancing an eraser on some part of his body; for example, "Can you turn around three times with an eraser on your head?"
3. The challenged player may answer "yes" or "no."
4. If he says "yes," he must do it to gain a point for his team (Team B).
5. If he says "yes," but cannot do it, the point goes to the challenger (Team A).
6. If he says "no," the challenger (Team A) can agree that the challenge is impossible and give the point to the opposition (Team B), or he can fulfill the challenge himself and gain a point for his own team (Team A).
7. Next, the first player on Team B asks the first player on Team A if he can do something while balancing an eraser, and so on as before.
8. The game continues in this way until each player has had a turn at challenging. To keep the game lively and interesting, *players may not repeat a challenge.*
9. All points are added and the team with the most points wins.

Goobing

SKILLS: FORMULATING QUESTIONS, SEQUENCING, LANGUAGE.

This game involves guessing an unidentified action by asking questions about how the action is performed.

Players: 5 to 12.
Materials: None.

Game Procedure
1. Players form a large circle.
2. A leader is chosen.
3. The leader thinks of an action, but does not tell the group. This unidentified action is called a "goob."
4. He commands players first to perform two specific actions, then to "goob"; for example, "Everyone clap your hands, everyone touch your head, everyone goob."

5. Since players cannot "goob" until they know what it means, they ask questions to find out how to do it. Questions must be answerable by "yes" or "no" and must be about how the action is performed, for example, "Do I use my hands to goob?"
6. Once a player has guessed what "goobing" is, he must repeat the first two actions the leader gave to the group, and then command the group to "goob," giving the correct action for "goobing."
7. If the player is correct, he becomes the new leader, thinks of a new "goob" and begins a new game.
8. If the player is incorrect, the present leader gets another turn.

Variations
As the game becomes easier, the leader may command more than two actions before the "goob."

14

The Mad Scientist

SKILLS: FORESEEING CONSEQUENCES, PLANNING, DETECTING IRREGULARITIES, GIVING AND FOLLOWING DIRECTIONS, LANGUAGE.

Players, or "robots," follow the commands of a leader, or "mad scientist," until he orders something impossible. The "scientist" must remember his commands to avoid contradicting himself, while players must recognize his contradictions.

Players: 5 to 12.
Materials: A large, brown paper bag with a drawing of a "mad scientist" on one side of it.

Game Procedure

1. One player is chosen as leader, or mad scientist. The scientist will specify where other players will be at the start and throughout the game.
2. The scientist begins the game by directing all of the robots, the rest of the players. The directions should include the entire group; for example, "Everyone sit at their desks," or "Everyone stand in front of the piano."
3. The scientist places the paper bag over his head so that he can no longer see his robots.
4. The scientist gives one robot a command; for example, "Robot Donna, stand up," or, "Robot Billy, walk forward until I say stop.... Stop!"
5. The orders require one action of one robot at a time.
6. A robot is not allowed to move unless commanded to do so.
7. Robots should walk stiff-limbed, in robot-like manner.
8. The scientist should speak in a loud, authoritative voice. This keeps the commands simple and insures that the voice is heard through the bag.
9. If a robot does not do exactly as he is told, without adding or omitting anything, the other robots call out, *"Ork!"* and the robot who made the mistake is ordered back to his starting point.
10. As soon as one robot has carried out a command, the scientist commands a different robot.
11. The scientist should change robots with each command so that all of the robots will get a turn.
12. He continues to give commands as long as each robot can follow the command given.
13. If the scientist gives a command that cannot be followed, for example, ordering a robot to walk forward when there is a table in the way, or ordering a robot to stand when he is already standing, the robot should say, *"Beep, beep, beep!"* which ends the game.
14. The robot and scientist then change places and the game begins again.

Special Considerations

In carrying out a command, a robot is likely to walk around things even though the command does not indicate that he should do so. While this may be caught by the other robots, it should be stressed that a robot can only do what he is told. One way of insuring this is to encourage the robots to look ahead to see if a command can actually be carried out, as given, before beginning to move.

A scientist may repeat the same command over and over again. This can be discouraged by requiring that the scientist neither call on the same robot twice in a row nor give the same order twice in a row.

If the game moves too slowly, two players may be chosen as scientists who alternate giving commands.

The game is best played in a rather small area, so that the scientist can get a better picture of where the robots are and where they could go, and so that the robots can hear the scientist.

London Bridge Catchall

SKILLS: GENERATING POSSIBILITIES, SPELLING.

In this version of "London Bridge," players do not sing the song, but words with a given letter may cause the bridge to fall.

Players: 5 to 12.
Materials: None.

Game Procedure

1. Two players are chosen to be a bridge, the *Its*.
2. One part of the bridge names a letter.
3. Players do not sing the song, "London Bridge," but begin to go under the bridge as they would in that game.
4. As each player goes under the bridge, he must stop, say a word that does not include the bridge's letter, count to three quickly, and move on.
5. Each player must say a word that has not been said before.
6. If a player's word has been said before or includes the bridge's letter, the bridge falls and captures the player.
7. Once a player is captured, all players sing a very quick chorus of "London Bridge Is Falling Down."
8. The captured player takes the place of the part of the bridge who named the letter.
9. The other half of the bridge names a new letter and the game begins again.

Special Considerations

If the players are poor spellers, an adult should monitor the game and correct players when necessary.

Last Letter—New Word

SKILLS: APPLYING RULES, SPELLING, WORD SKILLS.

Players must think of a word that begins the way another word ends.

Players: 5 to 12.
Materials: None.

Game Procedure

1. Players sit in a circle.
2. A player begins by saying a simple word.
3. The next player says a word that begins with the same letter as the last letter in the previous word. For example, if the first player said "house," the next player would have to think of a word that begins with *e*, such as "end."
4. The next player must think of a word that starts with the last letter of that word, and so on.
5. If a player cannot think of a word or makes an error, he must sit in the center of the circle until another child makes an error and changes places with him.
6. The game continues for as long as the players wish.

Special Considerations

With younger players, adult direction may be necessary the first few times the game is played to insure that mistakes are noticed.

17

Whatsit?

SKILLS: PERCEPTUAL ORGANIZATION.

Teammates try to recognize each other's drawings as they are being drawn.

Players: 11 (Can be adapted for more or less, depending on number of index cards.)

Materials: A pencil and several sheets of drawing paper for each player. Two identical decks of five index cards with one of the following printed on each card: dog, house, cup, boat, telephone. Decks should be replaced after each game. New cards should always name single objects that players could draw.

Game Procedure

1. One child is chosen as leader.
2. The remaining players form two equal teams.
3. The teams go to tables at opposite sides of the room. Drawing paper and pencils should be on the tables.
4. The leader stands between the teams. He holds one deck of cards for Team A and an identical deck for Team B.

5. When the leader says "Go!" one player from each team runs to him.
6. The leader shows each player the first card from their deck.
7. Each player runs back to his team and begins to draw the object named on the card.
8. As soon as a teammate thinks he recognizes the drawing (that is, the "whatsit") he writes its name on a piece of paper and takes it to the leader.
9. If he is wrong, the player returns to his team.
10. The first player continues his picture until someone guesses the correct object.
11 If a player guesses correctly, the leader shows the second player the next card from his team's deck and so on, as before.
12. The first team to complete its deck wins the game.

Duster

SKILLS: IDENTIFYING NEEDED INFORMATION, RECOGNIZING PROGRESS TOWARD A SOLUTION.

A leader chooses a secret object, then drops a dustcloth on the floor. Players try to find things that are closer than the dustcloth to the secret object.

Players: 5 to 12.
Materials: A dustcloth, piece of kleenex, or paper towel.

Game Procedure

1. One player is chosen as leader.
2. The other players stand in front of the leader.
3. The leader secretly chooses an object in the room and says, "I spy with my little eye something you can dust." The object must be something that players can touch.
4. He drops the dustcloth in the middle of the floor and calls on a player.
5. The player walks to an object, touches it, and asks, "Am I closer than the dustcloth?"
6. The leader says either, "Yes, so get the dustcloth and put it there," or "No, so sit down on the floor."
7. The dustcloth must get closer to the secret object each time it is moved.
8. Players who are told to sit on the floor are out of the game.
9. The leader calls on another player, and so on.
10. If no one has touched the secret object and all players are sitting on the floor, they all get up and continue the game.
11. The first player to touch the secret object is the winner and the leader for a new round.

19

Why — Because Charade

SKILLS: NONVERBAL COMMUNICATION, UNDERSTANDING CAUSE AND EFFECT.

Players use pantomime to match a cause with an effect.

Players: 10.

Materials: A set of ten index cards: five cause cards and five matching effect cards. One of the following should be printed on each card: Causes: You were very tired. You were very hungry. You went out on a cold and wet day. You ate too much. Someone was mad at you. Effects: You went to sleep. You ate a big meal. You caught a cold. You had a stomach ache. You were punched in the nose.

Cards should be used for two or three sessions, then replaced. The following provides an alternative set of cards:

Causes: You fell down the stairs. You were very thirsty. You were very bad. You slammed a door on your finger. You were out on a windy day.

Effects: You broke your leg. You drank a big glass of water. Your mother spanked you. You broke your finger. You mussed up your hair.

Game Procedure

1. Players form two equal groups (five in each group).
2. Each player in one group gets a cause card; each player in the other group gets an effect card. Tell the players in the effect group that their cards tell about some things that happened. Tell the players in the cause group that their cards tell why the things happened.
3. Players read silently, then act out the sentences on their cards, all performing at the same time.
4. As each player acts out his card, he watches the opposite group for the player (partner) who is acting out his matching cause or effect.
5. Players find their partners.
6. When all players have found a partner, each pair takes a turn acting out its cards for the rest of the group.
7. Partners compare cards to see if they have the right pair.

Find the Donkey

SKILLS: EDUCATED GUESSING, DETECTING IRREGULARITIES.

Players observe each other carefully to discover one player who is not actually taking part in the game.

Players: 10.
Materials: Nine index cards. One card is blank. Each of the other eight cards has a noun that can be represented by a sound effect printed on it. The following nouns are suggested: cow, dog, clock, cat, lamb, bee, train, and doorbell. A list of all eight nouns is needed for the leader.

Game Procedure
1. One player is selected as "caller" and given the cards and word list.
2. The leader gives each player one card, which is to be kept hidden.
3. The leader calls off the words quickly in any order, repeating as often as he likes.
4. As a word is called, the player who holds it makes its sound.

5. Players should not look at their cards during the game or reveal in any way that they actually have a word except to utter its sound when it is called.
6. All players try to "find the donkey" — the player with the blank card who does not make any sound.
7. The "donkey" should move his lips to try to fool the others.
8. The first player to "find the donkey" becomes caller and redistributes the cards for the next round.

Special Considerations
If the game is too easy, increase the number of players and add new cards. If the game is too hard, decrease the number of players and cards.

21

SKILLS: CLASSIFYING, DETECTING SIMILARITIES, LANGUAGE, READING.

Players try to think of objects that have a quality in common with three given objects.

Players: 5 to 12.
Materials: A set of index cards with a simple object on each card. The objects may be drawn or cut from coloring books and catalogs and pasted onto cards. The cards should be divided into sets of three so that all objects in a set have something in common. Although many others are possible, the following object sets are suggested: shoe, coat, pants (all clothing); scissors, needle, nail (all metal); bench, stool, chair (all used to sit on); guitar, violin, trumpet (all musical instruments); toothbrush, clothesbrush, hairbrush (all have handles or are used for brushing); iron, lamp, toaster (all have cords and plugs); igloo, cabin, teepee (all homes). Object sets should be replaced frequently.

Game Procedure
1. Players sit in a circle.
2. Each set of three cards is placed face-down in the center of the circle.
3. One player is chosen as leader.
4. The leader chooses one set of (three) cards.
5. He shows the cards to the rest of the group, then asks, "What things can you think of that match my cards?"
6. Players name as many different objects as they can that could go with the three cards. For example, if the cards pictured scissors, a nail, and a needle, players might name other sharp things.
7. The leader answers "yes" to any object named that matches his cards, and "no" to any that does not.
8. When the group can no longer name things, the leader calls on someone to tell how all of the things are the same. In the example, scissors, nail, and needle, a correct reply would be, "They are all sharp."
9. If a player guesses incorrectly, the leader calls on another player.
10. The player who guesses correctly becomes the new leader, picks another set of cards, and begins a new game.

Special Considerations
Players may need to be reminded not to tell how the objects are the same at first, but rather to name more things having that quality. They can only tell how they are the same at the end of a round when called on by the leader.

Clues

SKILLS: EDUCATED GUESSING, IDENTIFYING NEEDED INFORMATION.

Players must use all the clues given to guess an object the teacher or parent has in mind. Adult direction is necessary.

Players: 4 to 12.
Materials: None.

Game Procedure

1. Players divide into two teams and sit facing each other.
2. A player from each team gets paper and pencil to keep score for his team throughout the game.
3. The teacher writes *Clues* on one side of the chalkboard and *Guesses* on the other.
4. The teacher tells the players that he or she is thinking of an object in the room and that they are to guess what it is from the clues given.
5. The teacher gives a clue; for example, "It is long and thin."
6. The teacher writes the clue on the board under *Clues.*
7. The first player on Team A is asked to guess an object that will fit the clue.
8. The player guesses, then tells why he thinks so.
9. A good guess need not be the teacher's object, but it must fit the clue.
10. The group (both teams) decides if the player has made a good guess.
11. The teacher acts as a judge only in cases of dispute.
12. If the player makes a good guess, his team wins a point.
13. If the player makes a poor guess, the first player on Team B is asked to guess and so on as before.
14. Teams alternate giving guesses until a good guess is given and the point is won.
15. When a good guess is given, the teacher writes it on the board under *Guesses.*
16. He or she gives a second clue; for example, "It is made of wood."
17. The teacher calls on a player from Team B to begin guessing about the second clue.
18. The player must defend his guess in terms of both clues that have been given. As clues increase, players must justify answers in terms of all clues.
19. If a player guesses the object the teacher has in mind, he or she should try to change the object (without telling the players) so that the game may be carried on longer. For example, if the teacher's object is *bookshelf* and a player guesses it after the clues "long and thin" and "made of wood" the teacher might change the object to *pencil* so that a further clue, such as "It is small," would be required before players could guess the object.

20. Points increase with the number of clues. For example, if a player justifies two clues, his team wins two points, three clues, three points, etc.

21. If a player correctly guesses the object the teacher has in mind, and the teacher cannot think of another object to which he or she could change, the team gets double points, that is, twice the number of clues justified.

22. If four poor guesses are given in a row, the game ends and a new game begins. This usually indicates that players have too much information with which to deal.

23. When the teacher's object is guessed, both teams count their points and the team with the most points wins.

Variations

A variation of the game may be played in which the teacher thinks of an occupation that players must guess. It is best to use jobs that are well known by children, such as policeman, fireman, or bus driver, and clues that definitely describe or do not describe them. Avoid ambiguous clues. This variation of the game is more difficult for some players because it is more abstract. It is suggested that it be played after the first version has been introduced.

The Magazine Picture Game

SKILLS: CLASSIFYING, DETECTING SIMILARITIES, LANGUAGE.

Players win cards by making a statement about their own card that applies to the cards of as many players as possible.

Players: 5 to 12.
Materials: Thirty large index cards with a picture cut from a magazine and pasted onto each card. Cards may be prepared by the players before the game begins.

Game Procedure
1. Players sit on the floor in a circle.
2. One player is chosen to begin as dealer.
3. He deals one card to each player, including himself.
4. Each card is dealt face-up so that the players can see each other's cards.
5. The dealer begins the game by making a true statement about his own card, for example, "There is a man on my card."
6. If the statement is true of a player's card, he must give his card to the dealer.
7. The dealer collects all the cards he has "won" and places them in a pile behind him. These cards are no longer part of the game.
8. The dealer always leaves the card he originally dealt to himself face-up in front of him when he collects his winnings. It is not included in the cards he wins.
9. The deal is passed to the next player.
10. He deals a card only to the players who have lost a card, then makes a statement about his own card and so on, as before.
11. A statement may be made only once. Subsequent statements may mean the same as or be closely related to previous statements, but not identical.
12. Very general statements that easily include all cards are not acceptable, such as, "There is something in my picture," or "My picture is on a card."
13. The deal continues to be passed until each player has had a turn dealing and making a statement.
14. Each player counts the cards he has won and the player with the most cards is the winner.

Special Considerations
Although the winning and losing of cards usually keeps the group involved, it is wise to keep the number of younger players small (five to ten) to insure high interest.

The game may be made more difficult by increasing the number of players which also increases the number of synonyms and general statements required.

Occasionally, several players have lost the last card they were dealt and all of the cards have been used before each player has had a turn. If this happens, a player may request one card at random from any player's winning pile and use that card as if it were dealt to him.

SKILLS: CLASSIFYING, CODING, LANGUAGE.

Players must classify and code words quickly in order to stay in the game.

Players: 5 to 12.
Materials: None.

Game Procedure

1. Players stand in a circle.
2. One player is chosen to be *It* who stands in the middle of the circle.
3. *It* chooses two categories to be "zit" and "double zit." For example, any food could be "zit," any animal could be "double zit."
4. *It* begins to name things and points to each player, in turn, as he says a word.

5. After each word, *It* counts to five softly, to give the player time to think of an answer.
6. As *It* names things, each player must say "zit," for example, if a food is named; "zit-zit," for example, if an animal is named, or remain silent if something is named that does not belong to either category.
7. If a player answers incorrectly or fails to answer in time, he replaces *It*, names two new categories and begins a new game.

Special Considerations

Until the game has been played a few times, it may help players to write the two categories and their appropriate responses on the board for quick reference.

What Could Happen?

SKILLS: FORESEEING CONSEQUENCES, SEQUENCING, READING.

Players use their imaginations to develop a story about a specific situation.

Players: 5 to 12.

Materials: A set of ten index cards with one of the following situations printed on each card: Her mother is angry because Susan has spilled ice-cream all over her new dress. The teacher has caught the boys drawing silly pictures on the chalkboard when they should be doing their work. Sam and his dog are leaving muddy footprints all over the clean floor. Jane kicked the football and it crashed through the neighbor's picture window. Jim put all of his toys into the bathtub and the bathwater splashed all over the floor. Bill shot an arrow into Mr. Smith's tire and made it flat. Patty borrowed her mother's clothes and make-up, then made a mess of the bedroom. Debbie and Bob each have a dime for ice cream, but the ice cream truck has started to drive away. Mary's new kite has been blown into the highest branches of a tree. David likes peaches so much that he ate fifty of them today.

Game Procedure

1. Players sit in a large circle with five cards face-down in the middle.
2. One player begins by drawing a card from the deck.
3. He reads the card to the other players; for example, "Patty borrowed her mother's clothes and make-up, then made a mess of the bedroom."
4. The player tells what could happen; for example, "Her mother will scold her."
5. The player gets one point for a possible consequence.
6. The next player tells what could happen after that; for example, "Then her mother tells her to clean up the mess."
7. The player gets two points for a second possible consequence.
8. The next player tells what could happen after that.
9. If it makes sense and is not a repetition, he gets three points.
10. The game continues with a point added on each turn until a player cannot think of anything or repeats something.
11. The next player draws a new card, reads it to the other players and so on as before.
12. When all of the cards have been used, the player with the most points wins.
13. A new set of cards is used for the next game.

Variations

Once the game has been played, allow players to make up their own cards for the game. They should be told to write a sentence that tells about something interesting happening. Adult direction may be needed to insure that the sentences are clear to all players.

Special Considerations

If players have reading difficulties, it is suggested that an adult read the cards to the players during the game.

If the more able players seem to do all of the work in the game, group players according to their ability.

Yes, No, Maybe So

26

SKILLS: IDENTIFYING TRUTH, FALSITY, AND UNCERTAINTY, LANGUAGE.

Players look at a picture very carefully and determine whether comments made about the picture are true, false, or have nothing to do with what can be seen in the picture.

Players: 5 to 12.
Materials: Five different pictures that have plenty of objects and characters upon which to comment. Avoid choosing pictures from stories that the players know well so that the accuracy of a comment may be judged only from what is *seen*.

Game Procedure

1. A leader is chosen. For the first few rounds of the game, it is advisable for an adult to be the leader.
2. Players sit facing the leader.
3. The leader holds up a picture so that all players can see it.
4. The leader makes a statement about the picture.
5. He calls on one of the players to tell him if the statement he has made is true, not true, or if it is impossible to tell from the picture if the statement is true or not. A player's reply can be "yes," "no," or "maybe so, but I don't know."

The leader holds up a picture of animals in the woods. In one part of the picture is a robin sitting on a branch. The leader could say, "The robin is sitting on a branch," for which the correct answer would be "Yes." Or the leader could say, "The robin is flying near the tree." The correct answer would be "No." For "The robin is tired," the correct answer would be, "Maybe so, but I don't know."

6. If a player is wrong, the leader repeats the statement and calls on someone else.
7. The leader makes five different statements about the picture, following the same procedure.
8. Then he chooses a new leader who continues the game in the same manner with a different picture.

Special Considerations

The game may seem difficult at first, but with prompting from an older person and explanations of why an answer is incorrect, the players will soon catch on.

SKILLS: MAKING RULES, APPLYING RULES, ARITHMETIC.

Players make a rule about two playing cards, then try to find other cards that follow the rule.

Players: 4 to 12.

Materials: A deck of playing cards with the face cards and aces removed. A sheet of paper with a vertical line drawn down the middle. For more than eight players, add another deck of cards.

Game Procedure

1. Players sit around a table or in a circle on the floor.
2. One player begins as dealer.
3. He shuffles the cards and deals four to each player, face-up.
4. He places the sheet of paper in the middle of the table and deals two more cards on one side of it, face-up. These are called the "rule cards."
5. The dealer makes a rule that is true of the two rule cards, for example, both black; both red; one red, one black; both even; both odd; diamond and spade; two spades; five and two; seven and a smaller one; they add up to eight; both have the same number; one is three times bigger than the other; etc.
6. The dealer's rule will be used until there is a new dealer.
7. If possible, the dealer puts two of his cards on the other side of the sheet, then repeats the rule to show it is true of those cards.
8. The dealer must make a rule even if he can't think of one he could follow.
9. If the dealer cannot follow his rule, he passes.
10. If the player to the dealer's left has two cards that follow the rule, he repeats the rule and lays his cards on the other side of the sheet on top of any cards that are there.
11. If he doesn't have two cards that follow the rule, he passes.
12. If a player plays cards that don't follow the rule, the other players must tell him to take them back. Players should be reminded to watch for errors.
13. Players continue to take turns as before.
14. If everyone passes (because they cannot play any more cards that follow the rule), the player to the left of the dealer pulls the paper out from under the cards and places it on top of them.
15. The player to the left of the dealer becomes dealer, deals two new rule cards and makes a rule.
16. He does not deal new cards to each player. Each player keeps the cards he has left from the original deal and the game continues as before.
17. The first player to get rid of all his cards wins the game.

Red Rover

SKILLS: UNDERSTANDING CAUSE AND EFFECT, ORIGINALITY, LANGUAGE.

Players must think of something that would keep them from crossing over to the other team to avoid being captured.

Players: 4 to 12.
Materials: A set of index cards with one of the following on each card: sled, skis, sparrow, mouse, bicycle, horse, wagon, motorcycle, canoe, wheel, truck, elephant, bus, taxicab.

Game Procedure
1. Players divide into two equal teams.
2. Teams form two lines and face each other.
3. An imaginary line is drawn between the teams called the "because line."
4. Each player is given an index card.
5. The first player on Team A reads his card, for example, "wagon," then challenges the player across from him, "Red Rover, Red Rover, you're a 'wagon,' come over."
6. The challenged player must think of something that the "because line" could be that would keep him from coming over. For example, the person might say, "Because that's a roadblock and a wagon can't come over."
7. If the challenged player cannot think of something, or, as the game progresses, repeats another player, he is captured by the other team.
8. If the answer is satisfactory, he is not captured by the other team.
9. The same player then looks at his card, and proceeds to challenge the player who just challenged him.
10. When all players have exchanged challenges with a player on the opposite team, the team with the most captives wins.

Variations
Once players are familiar with the game, the cards may be omitted and players allowed to think of original things to call their opponents. If the game seems to move more quickly using the cards, players may print up their own cards before the game begins.

29

The "Er" Question Game

SKILLS: FORMULATING QUESTIONS, IDENTIFYING NEEDED INFORMATION, COMPARING, LANGUAGE, READING.

Players attempt to guess which of four pictured objects a leader has in mind by asking about an object only in comparison with the other objects.

Players: 5 to 12.

Materials: Two sets of index cards. One set should have one of the following comparative terms printed on each card: larger, thinner, brighter, taller, fancier, shorter, fatter, rounder, prettier, colder, softer, harder, sharper, clearer. The other set should have a picture of one of the following objects on each card: stocking, bow, pencil, fork, skunk, umbrella, boot, penny, piano, envelope, bathtub, thermometer, bowl, bus, tree, flower, cup, television, refrigerator, apple, barn, sink, dress, pen, bicycle, watch, safety pin, candle. The objects may be drawn or cut from coloring books and catalogs and pasted onto cards. If pictures of these objects are not available, other familiar objects may be used.

Game Procedure

1. A player is chosen as leader.
2. The other players form a semicircle facing the leader.
3. The leader chooses four cards from the deck of object pictures.
4. He sets the cards against the chalkboard ledge so that all players can see them.
5. He secretly chooses one of the objects for players to guess.
6. He passes each player one comparative term card.
7. Players take turns asking questions that can be answered "yes" or "no," and that include their comparative term. For example, if a player's card says, "taller," he might ask, "Is the thing you are thinking of taller than a tree?"
8. When all players have asked a question, the leader chooses one player to make a guess.
9. If the player can guess the correct object, he becomes the new leader.
10. If the player cannot guess the correct object, all players pass their cards to the right so that each of them has a new comparative term, then they begin to ask questions again.
11. The game continues until a player can guess the correct object.
12. The first player to guess correctly becomes the new leader, chooses four new picture cards, and the game begins again.

Readaround

SKILLS: COMPLETING AND CONTINUING, EDUCATED GUESSING,
USING CONTEXT IN READING.

A player must guess the next word in a sentence from the context of the previous words.

Players: 5 to 12.
Materials: A book with a suitable reading level for the players. They should not be already familiar with the book.

Game Procedure
1. Players sit in a circle.
2. One player is picked as the first reader.
3. She chooses a long sentence in the book and reads the first word.
4. The player to her left guesses the second word.
5. If the guess is wrong, the reader reads the first and second word, then the next player guesses the third word, and so on. For example, Reader: "The ...."
First child to the left: "boy."
Reader: "The animals ...."
Second child to the left: "had."
Reader: "The animals did...."
Third child to the left: "not."
Reader: "That's right, the animals did not say anything."

6. When a player guesses correctly, she becomes the new reader. The reader finishes the sentence then gives her the book.
7. She selects a sentence (not the next one), and so on, as before.
8. If a sentence is finished without anyone guessing a word correctly, the reader passes the book to the player on her left, who becomes the next reader, and so on.

Variations
Younger players sometimes prefer a version of the game in which more players may guess at each word. The rules are the same except that if the player is wrong, the next player guesses at the same word and so on until the word is guessed. If no one guesses, the reader gives the correct word and guessing begins on the next word.

31

SKILLS: ORIGINALITY, DEFINING, LANGUAGE, READING.

As players try to name things that are *not* used for a given purpose, the leader must tell how he *could* use those things in that way.

Players: 5 to 12.

Materials: A set of index cards with one of the following statements printed on each card: I'll use it to wrap a package. I'll use it to keep my money safe. I'll use it to get better when I'm sick. I'll use it to make a drink cold. I'll use it to cut a piece of paper. I'll use it to fix a rip in my coat. I'll use it to cut a piece of wood. I'll use it to paint a picture. I'll use it to hold a puppy. I'll use it to make myself look better. I'll use it to send a letter. I'll use it to keep some papers from blowing away. I'll use it to grow a garden. I'll use it to build a wagon. I'll use it to do my work at school. I'll use it to make my food hot. I'll use it to stick two pieces of paper together. I'll use it to clean house. I'll use it when I go to sleep. I'll use it to make light. I'll use it to make a loud noise. I'll use it to hold water. The cards should be replaced after the game has been played a few times. In making new cards, bear in mind that each card should state a specific use.

Game Procedure

1. The deck of statement cards is placed face-down on a table in front of the group.
2. One player is chosen as leader who stands before the group.
3. The leader draws the top three cards and reads them aloud.
4. The leader calls on volunteers, one at a time, to name objects.
5. Players should try to name objects that do not readily fit the uses on the leader's cards.
6. The leader must choose the most appropriate use (from only the three cards he has drawn) for each object named. He must think of a sensible way to fit each object into one of his uses.
7. If the leader's answer is not sensible, a player may ask him to either explain, "How?" or give up being the leader.
8. If a leader cannot think of an answer or justify his answer, the player who stumped him becomes leader, draws three cards and begins a new game.

Special Considerations
If a leader cannot read the cards, he may hold them up for the group to read together. If most of the players do not read well, one player may be chosen to draw and read the cards for each leader.

Players initially may have trouble recognizing that their job is to stump the leader. They may tend to name objects that fit easily into one of the leader's uses or actually to help the leader find appropriate uses. If so, they should be reminded not to help the leader and to name things that they do not think the leader can use.

Younger players may need adult guidance for several sessions. Since the game stimulates discussion, agreement, and disagreement, younger players may need to learn how best to resolve these discussions. A reasonable estimate is that a teacher or parent should play the game four times with second graders and three times with third graders before allowing them to play it independently.

SKILLS: GIVING AND FOLLOWING DIRECTIONS, LANGUAGE.

A player must duplicate a picture from another player's description.

Players: 4 to 12.
Materials: Large sheets of drawing paper and pencils or crayons.

Game Procedure
1. Each player gets a sheet of paper and a crayon.
2. Each player goes to a part of the room to draw a simple picture.
3. Finished pictures are placed face-down in a pile.
4. One player is chosen to be "artist."
5. The artist sits on the floor with all the other players behind her back in a semicircle.
6. A blank sheet of paper is placed in front of the artist.
7. One of the prepared pictures is placed behind the artist so that only the other players can see it.
8. Players take turns giving a direction to help the artist draw the picture on her blank paper. Directions should be clear enough that the artist can draw a picture as similar to the original as possible. For example, if the players are looking at a house, the first player could say, "Draw a long line going up and down." The next could say, "Draw three more lines so that you have a box." The next could say, "Put a door inside the box," and so on, until all parts of the house were described to the artist.

9. When players can think of no more directions to give the artist, the two pictures are compared and the artist chooses someone from the group to take her place with a new drawing.

Special Considerations
Players may need help at first in deciding what to tell the artist in order for her picture to look like the one they are describing. For example, they may need to be reminded of features in the picture they forgot to mention.

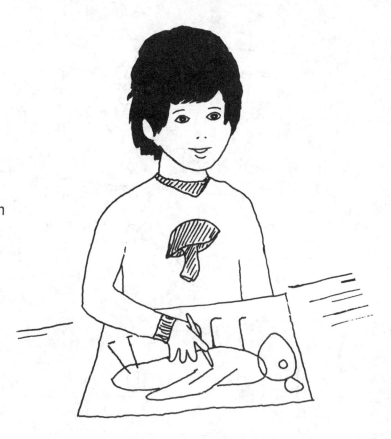

Wordaround

SKILLS: COMPLETING AND CONTINUING, SPELLING.

Players must add a new letter to an ongoing word without ending the word. It is similar to the spelling game, *Ghost*, but has a simpler scoring system.

Players: 5 to 12.
Materials: Paper and pencil for each player.

Game Procedure

1. Players sit in a circle on the floor.
2. Each player gets paper and pencil to keep his own score.
3. One player begins by giving the first letter of a word.
4. The next player continues the word by giving a possible next letter.
5. The next player continues with a possible next letter and so on.
6. Players should try to form as long a word as possible.
7. If a player unintentionally completes a word, it is considered complete even if he has another word in mind. For example, even if he is thinking of *soap* when he says *o* after *s*, the word *so* is complete.
8. Proper names are not acceptable.
9. A player gets one point for the 1st, 2nd, or 3rd letters of a word.
10. A player gets two points for the 4th, 5th, 6th, etc., letters of a word.
11. A player loses one point if he gives the last letter of a word.
12. Once a word is complete, the next player begins a new word.
13. If a player cannot think of a word that the previous letters could be a part of, he must challenge the previous players to name the word he had in mind.
14. If the challenged player does not have a real word in mind, he loses two points and the challenger begins a new word.
15. If the challenged player has a word in mind, the challenger loses one point and the next player begins a new word.
16. The first player to reach ten points wins the game.

Special Considerations

If the players are poor spellers, the game may be played with only three- or four-letter words.

Games for larger groups

Heads and Hips

SKILLS: CODING, APPLYING RULES, LANGUAGE.

Players must respond quickly at a given signal to become leader.

Players: 10 or more.
Materials: None.

Game Procedure
1. Players sit in a large circle.
2. A leader is chosen who stands in the center of the circle.
3. The leader spins around with his eyes closed.
4. At any time, he stops, opens his eyes, and puts his hands on either his head or his hips. He should decide where he will put his hands while he is spinning so that he can do so as soon as he stops.
5. If the leader puts his hands on his head, the player he is facing must immediately give his first name.
6. If the leader puts his hands on his hips, the player he is facing must immediately give his last name.
7. If the player gives the correct answer, he becomes leader.
8. If the player does not answer correctly, the leader gets another turn.

Variations
After the game has been played several times, another action may be added. For example, hands on head, say your first name; hands on hips, say your last name; hands on shoulders, say the name of the street you live on. More actions may be added if the players can handle them.

The response for a certain action may be changed to suit any lessons the teacher wishes to practice; for example, hands on head, name a plant; hands on hips, name an animal; or hands on head, name a country; hands on hips, name a city.

The Trolls

SKILLS: ORIGINALITY, GENERATING POSSIBILITIES.

Each player must cross an imaginary bridge in a different way to avoid becoming a troll.

Players: 10 or more.
Materials: None.

Game Procedure

1. Players form a long line at the start of an imaginary bridge.
2. Three players are chosen as trolls who sit at the end of the bridge.
3. Each player must cross the bridge in a way different from the players before him. For example, if the first player walks across the bridge, the second might skip, the third hop, and so on.
4. A player who repeats must change places with one of the trolls.
5. All players who cross the bridge successfully are winners.

Special Considerations

If players have trouble thinking of ways to cross, suggest that they pretend to move like different kinds of animals.

If the game is too easy, ask players to cross twice in two different ways.

Changing Things

36

SKILLS: DETECTING IRREGULARITIES, PLANNING, IMAGERY.

Players try to observe each other carefully enough to detect any changes in clothing, jewelry, or other characteristics.

Players: 10 or more.
Materials: None.

Game Procedure

1. Players form two equal teams.
2. The teams face each other.
3. Team A looks carefully at all players on Team B and tries to notice everything about them.
4. Team A leaves the room.
5. All members of Team B change at least one thing about themselves. For example, players may exchange shoes, remove a sweater, exchange jewelry, tuck in a shirt, remove glasses, unbutton something, put a pencil in a pocket, and so on.
6. Team A is called back into the room.
7. Team A faces Team B.
8. Starting at the beginning of the line, each player on Team A must mention a change in any player on Team B.
9. One point is given for each change noticed.
10. Team B then considers everything about players on Team A, leaves the room, and so on as before.
11. Points are added up and the team with the most points wins.

Variations

To include an entire class in this game, extra players who are not on a team may help the team that is changing things, offering ideas and exchanging various articles with the team members. This makes the changes more difficult to note and allows the players who are not on a team to become just as involved in the game.

SKILLS: STRATEGY.

Each team must figure out how to tag the opposition in a special way.

Players: 10 or more.
Materials: None.

Game Procedure

1. Players form two equal teams.
2. Each team appoints a leader.
3. Each team forms a line, or "snake," behind its leader.
4. Each player attaches herself to the teammate in front of her by putting her hands on the shoulders of that player.
5. If a player lets go of her teammate during the game, the game is forfeited to the opposing team.
6. Teams move to opposite sides of the room. If the game is played outside, teams should be about thirty feet apart.
7. To start the game, both teams must be facing the same direction with their leaders at the front of their lines, the lines straight, and all teammates holding onto each other.
8. Teams choose one of the leaders to say, "Go!"
9. Teams must wait motionless until the leader says, "Go!"
10. At "Go!" the leader of each team must try to touch the last player on the opposite team. The last player should try to avoid being touched and all other teammates should try to do whatever they can to help their leader and last player.
11. The first leader to tag announces that her team has won the game.

Secret Club

SKILLS: TESTING HYPOTHESES, IDENTIFYING NEEDED INFORMATION, DETECTING SIMILARITIES, FORMULATING QUESTIONS, LANGUAGE.

Players try to determine the two characteristics that a person must have in order to be in the leader's secret club.

Players: 10 or more.
Materials: None.

Game Procedure

1. A leader is chosen who stands in front of the group.
2. The leader thinks of two characteristics that some of the players have, for example, red hair and glasses, or blue clothing and running shoes.
3. She tells the group that there is a secret club and that some of them are in it because they have two special things about them.
4. The group asks questions, first to find out which of them are members of the club, and then to find out the two characteristics that constitute membership. The players' first questions will be about themselves, such as, "Am I in the club?" or "Is Judy in the club?" After a few members have been discovered, they will tend to ask questions about only one of the characteristics, for example, "Do they have glasses?"

It may take some time for them to ask a question that involves two characteristics, but the game is not won until they have done so. In the meantime, the leader should acknowledge the discovery of one characteristic but keep the lead until someone asks about both characteristics.
5. The leader calls on volunteers and answers one question at a time.
6. The leader can answer only "yes," or "no," but must answer truthfully.
7. The leader may not change the characteristics during the game.
8. Players identified as club members stand so that they may be seen by the entire group.
9. The first player to name both of the characteristics necessary for membership in the secret club becomes the leader and the game begins again.

Special Considerations
If finding two characteristics is too difficult, a simple version of the game may be played in which only one characteristic is necessary. If the game is too easy, three characteristics may be required.

Variations

Occasionally, players tend to put an emphasis on being in the club rather than on discovering the concepts involved. If this is the case, a different version of the game may be played that gives the players more choices. Each player holds up an object for the leader. The leader selects characteristics of the objects rather than the players. If a player is told that she is not in the club, she may change objects and try again. If it is difficult to find a sufficient variety of objects, picture cards with simple objects may be used. In this version of the game, it is important to impress upon the leader that her secret should be two things *about* the objects, not the name of the object. While the game requires a good deal of direction when it is introduced, it is learned very quickly. Even with first grade players, it is unlikely that they will need help in playing the game again.

"ARE THE KIDS IN THE CLUB WEARING SOMETHING BROWN?"

The Witch's Captives

39

SKILLS: CLASSIFYING, GENERATING POSSIBILITIES.

Players must name members of a category that the witch has not yet named in order to avoid becoming her captive.

Players: 10 or more.
Materials: None.

Game Procedure
1. Players sit in a circle.
2. One child is chosen as "witch" and stands outside the circle.
3. The witch chooses a category of things for all of the players to belong to, such as all animals or all clothing. The players and the witch maintain the same category throughout the game.
4. The witch names as many members of the category as she can; for example, "Are there any cats here? Are there any horses here? Are there any dogs here?" and so on.
5. Players do not answer the witch, but each must try to think of a member of the category that the witch has not mentioned.
6. When the witch cannot think of anything else, she gives up.
7. Once the witch has given up, each player takes a turn telling the witch what he or she is.
8. Each player must be a different member of the witch's category.

9. The witch may take any player who (1) cannot think of anything, (2) names something the witch named, (3) names something already named by another player, or (4) names something that does not belong to the witch's category.
10. Captives must leave the circle and go to another part of the room designated by the witch.
11. When each player has had a turn, a new witch is chosen from the players who have not been captured and the game begins again.
12. Each new witch should be encouraged to think of a category that has not been used in previous games.

Special Considerations
Some witches are quite slow in naming things. Others are reluctant to give up. This can slow the game to a halt. One way to avoid the problem is to teach the children a whispered chant: "Slow witch, slow witch, must give up." If the players have time to give this chant, the witch must stop.

The witch may name a category with very few members, such as colors or shapes. This is actually a good strategy in that it insures more captives since the players will probably be unable to come up with any more than the witch does.

40

Mimic

SKILLS: EDUCATED GUESSING, DETECTING IRREGULARITIES.

In this game of follow-the-leader, players must find the leader.

Players: 10 or more.
Materials: None.

Game Procedure
1. Players form a large circle.
2. One player is chosen to be *It* who leaves the room.
3. A leader is chosen.
4. The leader begins to perform actions as the group follows.
5. Players should be told that they will be trying to fool *It*, and to try not to be obvious about how they watch the leader as they mimic her.
6. The leader should be told to change her actions often and to make changes when *It* is not looking at her.
7. *It* is called back into the room.
8. The leader continues to perform different actions with the rest of the group mimicking her.
9. *It* must look carefully to determine who the leader is. *It* should be prompted on things to look for, such as, "Who do the players seem to be looking at?" and "Who seems to be doing a different action first?"
10. *It* is given three guesses to find the leader.

11. If *It* guesses correctly, the leader becomes *It* and leaves the room.
12. If *It* guesses incorrectly all three times, *It* remains *It*, leaves the room and the game begins again.

Variations
The game may be made more difficult by having all players remain at their desks to play. *It* stands at the front of the room to determine the leader.

Not-So-Musical Chairs

SKILLS: PLANNING, WORD SKILLS.

There is no music in this version of musical chairs and players must have a particular reason for seeking a particular chair.

Players: 9 or more.
Materials: Small chairs equal to one third of the total number of players; a pencil and several index cards for each player.

Game Procedure

1. Chairs are placed in a small circle with their backs to the inside.
2. One-third of the players are chosen to stand inside the circle of chairs, one behind each chair.
3. The rest of the players form a large circle around the chairs and players.
4. Players inside the circle decide on the type of words that must match theirs throughout the game. Examples might be rhyming words, words that mean the same, opposites, or words with the same beginning sound.
5. Each player inside the circle says a word. Every word must be different and of the type specified.
6. Each player inside the circle writes his word on a card and puts it face-down on his chair.
7. The players inside the circle slowly count off. This gives the other players some time to think.
8. Players in the outer circle must think of a word that goes with one (or more) of the inner players' words in the way

specified and remember which player said it. For example, if rhyming words were specified and the inner players said "dog, mouse, bat," then the outer player might think of log, house, or cat, and keep in mind which inner player the word goes with.
9. As soon as the counting stops, each outer player tries to be first to sit in the chair of the inner player whose word he thinks he matches.
10. Players sit on a chair and a card. They may not look at the card.
11. In turn, each seated player asks if his word is correct.
12. If the inner player says the word is correct, the seated player takes over that chair for the next round.
13. If the inner player says the word is incorrect, he proves it by showing the card, sends the seated player back to the outer circle and keeps the chair for the next round.

Special Considerations

Some players are too slow to reach a chair first. One way to give these players a better chance is to change all inner players for each new game. When a seated player is incorrect, the inner player would call on an unseated volunteer to give a word and replace him in the inner circle.

If the game seems too easy, players may wish to change the type of words required for each new round.

42

Name Six

SKILLS: GENERATING POSSIBILITIES, WORD SKILLS.

In this version of "Hot Potato," players think of six words with the same beginning letter before an object passes around the circle.

Players: 10 or more.
Materials: A small object that can be passed around the circle.

Game Procedure
1. Players form a large circle.
2. One player is chosen to sit in the center of the circle.
3. The center player closes her eyes while the other players quickly pass an object around the circle.
4. At any time, the center player claps her hands and opens her eyes.
5. At the clap, the player with the object must keep it.
6. The center player names any letter except *x*, *y*, or *z*.
7. The player with the object starts to pass it around the circle, then names six things that start with the center player's letter. For example, if the center player said *a*, the player holding the object would pass it on, then might quickly say, "apple, arm, ant, art, ask, ash," before the object comes back to her.

8. She must name all six before the object returns to her.
9. If she succeeds in naming six things in the time allowed, the center player must remain there for another round.
10. If the player cannot name six things in the time allowed, she takes the center player's place for the next round.

Special Considerations
If it is too difficult for players to think of six things beginning with the same letter in such a short period of time, the required number of words can be lowered to as few as three.

As the players become more adept at the game, they may purposely name less than the required number of words in order to have a turn in the center of the circle. It should be emphasized that the idea of the game is to outwit the center player, *not* to go to the center.

Which One Am I Thinking Of?

43

SKILLS: FORMULATING QUESTIONS, IDENTIFYING NEEDED INFORMATION, LANGUAGE.

Players ask questions to guess which of four objects the leader has in mind.

Players: 10 or more.

Materials: Forty index cards with a familiar, single object on each card. Objects may be cut from coloring books or catalogs and pasted onto cards. Pictures of the following and/or similar objects are recommended: lamp, bed, typewriter, squirrel, pigeon, toaster, shovel, hammer, flashlight, cup, kettle, saw, knife, pen, pencil, dollar bill, comb, screwdriver, pail, toothbrush, nail, book, telephone, clock, spoon, watch, fork, basket, scissors, candle, brush, spool of thread, letter, stamp, iron, broom, duck, chicken, etc.

Game Procedure

1. One player is chosen as leader.
2. The leader picks four object cards and sets them on the chalkboard ledge so that all of the players can see them.
3. She chooses one card but does not tell the group which one.
4. She asks the group, "Which one am I thinking of?"
5. Players ask questions about the four objects to figure out which one the leader is thinking of.
6. Questions must be answered "yes" or "no." For example, if the pictures are cup, flashlight, hammer, and shovel, a player could ask, "Is it used to dig?"
7. After four questions, the leader calls on someone to guess her object.
8. If a player guesses correctly, she becomes the new leader, chooses four new cards, and the game begins again.
9. If no one can guess the answer, the leader takes four new cards and begins the game again.

Special Considerations

If the game is too easy, allow only three questions before players guess at the object.

Make a Puzzle

SKILLS: PERCEPTUAL ORGANIZATION.

This is a team game in which each team makes puzzles for the opposite team to reconstruct.

Players: 10 or more.
Materials: Scissors and a blank sheet of paper for each player.

Game Procedure

1. Each player gets a pair of scissors and a blank sheet of paper.
2. Players form two equal teams with opponents paired off and facing each other.
3. Each player cuts his paper into four pieces, then shuffles the pieces.
4. One player is appointed to say "Go!"
5. When the player says "Go!" opposing pairs exchange and reconstruct each other's puzzles. Be sure that all players have completed cutting and shuffling their puzzles before the exchange is made. Players should reconstruct the puzzles as quickly as possible.
6. The team that reconstructs all of its puzzles first, wins the game.

Special Considerations

If the game is too easy, increase the number of pieces a puzzle may have to five, six, or more.

If the game is too difficult, decrease the number of pieces a puzzle may have to three.

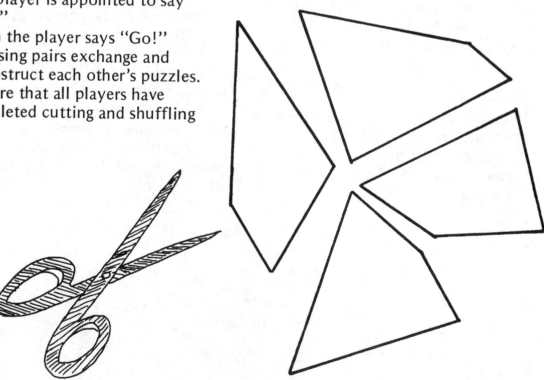

Alphabet Questions

45

SKILLS: FORMULATING QUESTIONS, DESCRIBING, LANGUAGE.

Players solve alphabet questions presented by their opposition. The game requires an understanding of beginning letters and simple descriptions.

Players: 8 or more.
Materials: Twenty-four index cards with a different letter of the alphabet on each card (excluding *x* and *z*); a piece of paper with a vertical line down the middle.

Game Procedure

1. Players form two equal teams and line up on opposite sides of a table.
2. The letter cards are shuffled and spread out on the table, face-down.
3. The piece of paper is placed on the table so that the vertical line divides the teams.
4. The first player on Team A turns over a card, for example, *d*.
5. She makes up a question for the first player on Team B; for example, "What starts with *d* that can bite?"
6. The first player on Team B answers. In the case above, she might say "dog."
7. The answer does not have to be the one the asker has in mind as long as it is reasonable and starts with the correct letter.
8. If the answer is correct, the first player on Team B takes the card and puts it on her team's half of the paper.
9. The first player on Team B takes a new card and makes up a question for the first player on Team A, and so on.
10. If a player cannot answer, her teammates may help her.
11. If no one on the team can answer, the player says, "We give up."
12. When a team gives up, the asker must give the answer she had in mind, then her team wins the card.
13. If the asker cannot answer her own question, she must give the card to the opposition.
14. The second player on Team B takes a new card and makes up a question for the second player on Team A and so on, as before, until each player has had a turn asking and answering.
15. If a player gives a word that starts with an incorrect letter or that does not answer the question, the other team must tell what is wrong with it. The card is then placed face-down on the table again.
16. The game stops when all of the cards have been won.
17. The team that has the most cards on its half of the paper wins the game.

SKILLS: CLASSIFYING, GENERATING POSSIBILITIES, WORD SKILLS.

Players use beginning sounds in alphabetical order to answer a question.

Players: 10 or more.

Materials: Ten index cards with one of the following questions printed on each card: What animals live in a zoo? What do you find in a house? What do you find in school? What names are given to girls? What names are given to boys? What do people eat for supper? What clothes do people wear? What things are used to cook with? What things are used to build with? What toys do children play with?

Game Procedure

1. Players sit in a circle.
2. One player is chosen as leader who sits in the circle with the cards.
3. The leader draws a card and reads it aloud; for example, "What animals live in a zoo?"
4. The leader points to a player who must answer the question with one word beginning with *a*. The next player must answer with a word beginning with *b*. The next player answers with a word

beginning with *c*, and so on through the alphabet. For example, the first player might say "*a*pe," the second, "*b*uffalo," the next, "*c*amel," the next, "*d*eer," etc.

5. If a player cannot think of a word, she asks the leader to tell her.
6. If the leader says a word, she keeps the lead and the next player continues the game.
7. If the leader cannot say a word, she asks if anyone else can answer.
8. If no one says a word, the letter is skipped and the game continues with the next letter. This avoids the problem of impossible examples, such as, food that begins with *x*.
9. If a player answers after the leader fails to, she becomes the leader and draws a card for a new game.

Pattern Relay

SKILLS: SEQUENCING, GENERATING POSSIBILITIES.

Players must repeat a series of actions that a leader performs.

Players: 8 or more.
Materials: Objects found in the classroom or home.

Game Procedure

1. Players divide into two equal teams.
2. Each team chooses a leader who will lead the opposing team.
3. The chosen leaders go over to the opposing team.
4. Teams form two lines and face each other.
5. A large area should be left between the two teams.
6. Each leader chooses four objects and places them in a line in front of the team she is leading. In other words, the two teams are lined up facing each other with a row of four objects in front of each team.
7. Teams play the game at the same time.
8. Another player is appointed to say, "Go!"
9. When the player says "Go!" each leader goes down the line of objects and does something with each object in any order. For example, one leader may have lined up a chair, a book, a jacket, and a chalkboard eraser.

She might pick up the book, sit in the chair, balance the eraser on her head, and finally throw the jacket over her shoulder.
10. When the leader is finished, the first player on a team tries to repeat the leader's pattern exactly.
11. If a player can do this correctly, the leader must create a new pattern with the same objects for the next person on the team.
12. If the player cannot repeat the pattern correctly, the leader repeats the pattern, and the same player must try again.
13. The pattern remains the same and the same player must try to repeat it until she can do it correctly before the next team member may have a turn. Leaders, of course, try to trick the team they are leading as they are the opposition.
14. The first team whose players correctly repeat all of the patterns they are shown wins the game.

Special Considerations

Leaders may tend to make the patterns too easy at first. It should be emphasized that the pattern is for the opposing team and that the leader should try to trick them if possible.

48 Rhyming Riddle Relay

SKILLS: FORMULATING QUESTIONS (RIDDLES), DESCRIBING, LANGUAGE.

Each player must answer a riddle posed by a teammate, but the answer must rhyme with a word that accompanies the riddle.

Players: 10 or more; may be adapted for less.
Materials: None.

Game Procedure

1. Players face each other or form two equal teams and stand in two lines.
2. Teams play at the same time.
3. The first player on each team asks her next teammate to

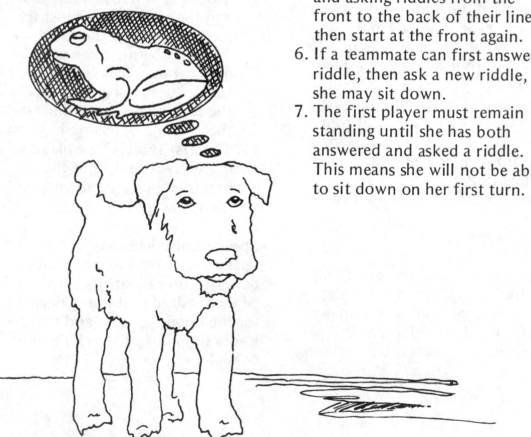

solve a rhyming riddle. A rhyming riddle is a simple descriptive statement about a word that rhymes with the object of the riddle. For example, "I'm thinking of a pet that rhymes with log," (dog), or, "I'm thinking of something that's found in the kitchen and it rhymes with pink," (sink), etc.

4. The teammate must solve the riddle and think of a new riddle for the next teammate and so on.
5. Teammates take turns answering and asking riddles from the front to the back of their line, then start at the front again.
6. If a teammate can first answer a riddle, then ask a new riddle, she may sit down.
7. The first player must remain standing until she has both answered and asked a riddle. This means she will not be able to sit down on her first turn.

8. Once a riddle has been asked, it must be answered before the asker can sit down. This may mean that if no one can answer the riddle, it will be passed along until the original asker gets another turn. If so, she must answer her own riddle to sit down.

9. If a player's riddle is inaccurate in any way, she must remain standing; for example, a word that doesn't rhyme, an inaccurate descriptive statement, or incorrect information.

10. If a player answers but cannot ask a new riddle, the next player can only ask and will not be able to sit down until she gets another turn to do both.

11. A player should pass quickly if she cannot answer or ask.

12. A player must accept a true solution to her riddle even if it is not the one she had in mind. For example, "An animal that rhymes with mat," could be answered "rat," even though the asker had "cat" in mind.

13. A player's part in the relay is over as soon as she sits down.

14. The first team with only one player standing wins the game.

Special Considerations

Younger players may not be able to generate riddles very well, making the pace of a relay too slow. If so, a leader (no teams) may be chosen to ask a riddle. The player who answers it correctly becomes the leader, asks a new riddle and so on.

If players have particular difficulty generating riddles when the game is introduced, an older person should help them with step-by-step instructions: "First think of something, but don't say it. Now say one thing *about* it. Now tell us a word it rhymes with."

Players may give a nonsense word as a rhyme; for example, "It has wheels and it rhymes with *sus*," (bus). Since this is better than a real word that does not rhyme, nonsense rhymes may be acceptable at first. Then players should be encouraged to use real rhyming words.

With older players, it may appear that the teams do not or cannot trust each other. If so, each team may assign a monitor to the opposing team.

While some players may be sitting through most of the relay, the game goes quickly and the players usually remain interested. If restlessness occurs, the team size should be reduced so that lengthy waiting is eliminated.

49 Secret Club Word Game

SKILLS: TESTING HYPOTHESES, IDENTIFYING NEEDED INFORMATION, DETECTING SIMILARITIES, FORMULATING QUESTIONS, WORD SKILLS.

Players ask questions to find the qualities a word must have to be in a secret club.

Players: 10 or more.

Materials: A set of index cards with one of the following words on each card: at, in, on, of, ate, and, off, end, sing, ring, the, an, he, she, me, be, her, him, them, cat, dog, pig, can, thing, that, tree, try, cry, dry, pail, mail, rail, some, come, meat, seat, gate, girl, boy, toy, toe, top, tap, pat, rain, silly, stamp, sting, safe, drop, street, mouse, house, horse, cow, how, now, wing, nose, rose, pan, pen, pin, sheet, shirt, skirt, dress, hair, rat, man, men, bring, take, give, live, turn, burn, sink, ink, barn, farm, sheep, sleep, bat, ten, five, stick, tack, pack, pick, park, dark, do, king, day, dig, tell, say.

Materials may be made by the players if they wish to choose and print words onto cards. Flash cards also may be used. Older players may wish to use longer words.

Game Procedure

1. One player is chosen as leader who stands before the group.
2. The leader gives each player a word card to hold up.
3. The leader secretly thinks of something that some of the words have in common, for example, an *s* in them, a *t* at the end, a double letter, or an *ai* in the middle.
4. She tells the group that some of them are in her secret word club because their words look alike in some special way.
5. Players ask questions, first to find out which of them are in the club, and then to find out how the words in the club are alike. At first, players will ask about themselves and others; for example, "Am I in the club?" "Is Amy?" Once a few club members are identified, they will begin to ask questions about the words. If players notice something similar about the words that the leader has not intended, she should tell them that it is true but it is not the special thing about her club.
6. The leader calls on volunteers and answers one question at a time.
7. She must answer all questions truthfully and may answer only "yes" or "no."
8. The leader may not change her club criterion during the game.
9. Players identified as having words in the club go to the front of the group and hold their cards so that the entire group may see them.
10. Club members are not told why they are in the club so that they too may try to figure it out.

11. The first player to figure out why the words are in the club becomes the new leader and the game begins again.

Variations

Once the game has been introduced, a choice-of-cards version may be played. Some players enjoy being in the club as much as they enjoy discovering the reason for it. Players may expand their chances of club membership and test their hypotheses about membership by being given three, four, or even five cards (avoid two) instead of one. Each player would hold up a card, as before, and ask if the word belongs in the club. If it does not, the player may turn the card face-down and try again with one of the remaining cards, etc., until she makes a correct judgement. This version requires three, four, or five times as many cards as players. Players whose words are identified as being in the club would not be allowed to ask questions about the words in this version.

Special Considerations

If the game is too easy, the leader may notice two things about the words and use both; for example, "They start with *s* and have double letters." A player must know both things to become leader.

When the game is introduced, the first few leaders may tend to use the same criterion, such as the beginning letter of the words. This may be avoided if an adult is the leader for two or three games and uses a new criterion for each game: first, the ending letter; next, the number of letters; and then, double letters. Each new leader should be encouraged to think of a new criterion for her club.

Reading is not essential to play the game. In fact, with readers it may be necessary to stress that the words in the club *look alike* in order to avoid guessing at other relationships, such as categories, parts, and uses. Letter recognition, however, is necessary.

While the game loses much of its thinking value for players above the third grade, it has considerable potential as a spelling skill-builder for older players. Many more and varied words could be added for use by these players so that a leader could choose from criteria involving larger portions of the words, such as, prefixes, suffixes, rhyming words that are or are not spelled alike, syllabification, number of vowels or consonants.

Count and Clap

SKILLS: SEQUENCING, ARITHMETIC (MULTIPLES OF NUMBERS).

This game requires the ability to count by 2s, 3s, 4s, and so on.

Players: 10 or more.
Materials: None.

Game Procedure

1. Players form a large circle.
2. One player is chosen to be *It* and stands in the middle of the circle.
3. *It* chooses a number that the group can count by.

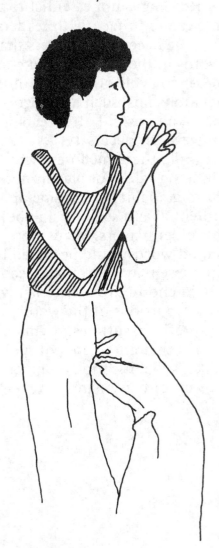

4. Players count off around the circle.
5. When a number comes up that is divisible by the number *It* chose, the person who should say that number must clap instead. For example, if the leader chose the number 3, players would count off around the circle as follows: "1, 2," *clap*, "4, 5," *clap*, "7, 8," *clap*, and so on.
6. If a player makes a mistake, he replaces *It* and chooses a new number.
7. Players begin counting off again, beginning with 1 and so on, as before.

Special Considerations

With younger players it is advisable to play the game by clapping for all the odd numbers or all the even numbers.

If players have a weak grasp of number facts, begin the game with 2, 5, or multiples with which they are familiar.

If the game is too easy, players may be told to clap on any number that is divisible by *It*'s number or that includes *It*'s number. For example, if the number is 3, players would clap on 3, 6, 9, 12, 13, 15, etc.

Say It Another Way

SKILLS: PARAPHRASING, LANGUAGE.

Each player repeats something another player has said by changing the words but not the meaning.

Players: 10 or more.
Materials: None.

Game Procedure

1. One player is chosen to keep score.
2. The other players divide into two equal teams with opposing players lined up and facing each other.
3. The first player on Team A tells the first player on Team B to do something, for example, "Touch your nose."
4. The first player on Team B performs the action and tells the first player on Team A to do the same thing, but he must give the command using different words (say it another way); for example, "Put your finger on your nose."
5. If both players perform correctly, both teams get a point.
6. If the player on Team B cannot say the same thing in different words, only Team A gets a point.
7. The game continues with Team A players telling Team B to do something, Team B players doing it, and then saying it another way.

8. At the end of the lines, the procedure reverses so that Team B players tell Team A players to do something, Team A players do it, and then say it another way.
9. At the end of the game, the team with the most points wins.

Special Considerations
With young players, it may be necessary to practice changing the words in a command without changing the meaning before the game is played so that it will move quickly once it has begun.

52

SKILLS: SEQUENCING, APPLYING RULES.

One player must discover the pattern of actions performed by the other players.

Players: 10 or more.
Materials: None.

Game Procedure
1. Players form a circle.
2. One player is chosen to be leader.
3. The leader chooses a player to be *It*.
4. *It* leaves the room.
5. The leader has the players count off to a given number around the circle, for example, "1, 2, 3; 1, 2, 3;" etc.
6. The counting off should not exceed five.
7. The first "1" performs an action that will be the action for all "1s." The first "2" performs an action for all "2s." The next player performs an action for all "3s," and so on, depending upon the number to which they counted off. Thus all "1s" might put their hands on their heads; all "2s," put their fingers on their noses; all "3s," touch their toes, etc. Players should act quickly while *It* is out of the room.
8. The leader says, "All together — Go!" and all players perform their actions at the same time. This is a practice before *It* returns.
9. *It* returns and stands in the circle.
10. When she chooses, she says, "All together—Go!" and the players perform their specified actions only once, and all at the same time.
11. *It* may say "All together—Go!" three times as she tries to find out how many actions there are.
12. After three "Go!s," she must point to a player, then say and do the following: "*You* did this," and perform that player's action, then point to another player and say, "So *you* will do this," and perform the actions performed by the next players, until each of the actions is shown.
13. If *It* is correct, she chooses a new *It* and begins a new game as leader.
14. If *It* is wrong, the leader chooses a new *It* and begins a new game.
15. The number of actions assigned during a game should always differ from that of the previous game.

Store

SKILLS: CLASSIFYING, LANGUAGE.

Two teams check each other's ability to set up a specialized store.

Players: 8 or more.
Materials: A large, blank sheet of paper and a pencil for each team, and twenty tokens.

Game Procedure

1. Players form two equal teams.
2. Teams go to separate parts of the room to prepare for the game.
3. Each team decides on the type of store it "owns," and makes a list of things, or "stock," that its store sells. Teams should try to include everything on the list that such a store would have. At this time, a team leader may be chosen to write the list as teammates suggest items and to check the list and hold tokens for the team during the game.
4. Once the lists are completed, teams line up and face each other.
5. Each team gets ten tokens.
6. The teams tell each other the kind of store they "own."
7. Teams take turns asking the opposition for items it should have in its store. They cannot ask for something that would not be found in that type of store.
8. If a team has an item asked for on its list, it wins a token from the team that asked.
9. If a team does not have an item asked for on its list, it loses a token to the team that asked.
10. The first team to win all the tokens, wins the game.

Special Considerations

If the game seems too long, teams may count their tokens after all players have had one turn. The team with the most tokens wins the game.

54

Tell and Spell

SKILLS: DEFINING, SPELLING.

Players try to guess the word that the leader is describing, then prove their guess by the spelling of the word.

Players: 16 to 26.
Materials: A set of twenty-six index cards with one capital letter of the alphabet on each card, and a set of twenty-six blank index cards.

Game Procedure

1. One player is chosen as leader.
2. The leader gives each player one alphabet card and one blank card.
3. The leader secretly chooses a word and writes it on a small piece of paper. She keeps the piece of paper well concealed from all players throughout the game.
4. She describes the word as fully as possible to the other players. For example, if the leader chooses "elephant," she might say, "It's a large animal that lives in Africa."
5. Each player tries to figure out what the word is.
6. When a player thinks she knows the word, she does not raise her hand to guess, but looks to see if her alphabet letter is in the word she thinks the leader is describing.
7. If so, she writes the word on the back of her card, then goes to the front of the room and holds up her letter. Players

should write their word very small so that no one will see it. This simply insures that players actually have a word in mind.

8. When all players who think they have a letter in the word are standing at the front of the room, the leader tells those who have incorrect letters to return to their seats.
9. The leader also names any missing letters but does not tell what they are.
10. If letters are missing, time is given for players to reconsider the word.
11. The leader tells players whose letter appears twice in the word to print their letter again on their blank card and hold it up.
12. Once these corrections and additions have been made, the leader calls on a player who is not at the front of the room to guess the word.
13. If the player guesses correctly, players at the front of the room put the letters in the correct order and the player who guessed becomes the new leader.
14. If the player does not guess correctly, the leader says the word, the players at the front of the room put the letters in the right order, and the leader begins a new game.

Index

NOTE: THIS INDEX REFERS TO THE SKILL BY GAME NUMBER.